*What a pleasure to find a book that actually delivers what is promised! **Embrace Prosperity** is clear, concise and very helpful. I highly recommend it.*
Zoilita Grant, Hypnotic Coach (US)

Rapid Relief with Logosynthesis®

Embrace PROSPERITY

RESOLVE BLOCKS TO EXPERIENCING ABUNDANCE

DR. LAURIE WEISS
DR. WILLEM LAMMERS

Empowerment Systems Books

Embrace Prosperity

Resolve Blocks to Experiencing Abundance

Rapid relief with Logosynthesis®

Laurie Weiss, Ph.D

Willem Lammers, DPsych

2020 Laurie Weiss. All rights reserved. No part of this book may be reproduced in any written, electronic, recording or photocopying form without written permission of the publisher except for the use of brief quotations in a book review.

All Rights Reserved.

ISBN 978-1-949400-21-2 (paper)

ISBN 978-1-949400-22-9 (ebook)

ISBN 978-1-949400-23-6 (audio)

Library of Congress Control Number: 2020901321

Publisher

Empowerment Systems Books

506 West Davies Way

Littleton, CO 80120 USA

Phone 303.794.5379

LaurieWeiss@EmpowermentSystems.com

www.EmpowermentSystems.com

Books may be purchased in quantity by contacting the publisher directly.

Cover design: Nick Zelinger, NZGraphics.com

Logosynthesis® is a registered trademark,
owned by Willem Lammers in Maienfeld, Switzerland.

ADVANCED PRAISE

As a seasoned wealth advisor, I thoroughly enjoyed reading **Embrace Prosperity** *as a book that clearly illustrates many of the real-life experiences around money that I have seen my clients face. The author's recognition of these issues, with follow up guidelines on how to address, delivers to the reader some practical guidance around the very important subjects of wealth management.*

**Mark J. Smith, CPA/PFS, CFP, CIMA Principal,
M.J. Smith and Associate (US),
Forbes Top 250 Wealth Advisors 2019**

Embrace Prosperity *provides the easiest way to move from money worries to money freedom. It's for those for whom lack of money is a daily, ongoing anxiety. And it's for those who only worry about money occasionally, perhaps at the end of the month when the bills are due. The key lies with just the few words of the Logosynthesis process. Dr. Laurie*

Weiss, a certified Logosynthesis practitioner and Dr. Willem Lammers, who created the process, have written a book that explains money. It offers tools to help readers understand their own beliefs and habits around money: the energy of money, how we get into money traps, and how to get out of them. The book is full of engaging case studies plus valuable check lists, worksheets, and directions for using Logosynthesis by harnessing the power of a few words. I've read dozens of money books: **Embrace Prosperity** *is the top of my list.*

MaryJo Wagner, PhD, (US)
Author, *Finding My Hero*

I thoroughly enjoyed reading Embrace Prosperity as Laurie Weiss and Willem Lammers team up to demonstrate an innovative approach to wellness—Logosynthesis®. Highlighting their separate stories about how they were able to shift from feelings of scarcity to feelings of abundance allowed me to recognize habitual patterns in my life that no longer serve me. I was trained to set goals to measure my progress towards abundance and when I achieved my goal, there was always a new measure. As Laurie and Willem highlight, abundance is more than something to measure. It is a feeling. As a practitioner in Logosynthesis®, I have come to appreciate the power in working with this simple yet powerful technique to allow me and others to enjoy life more fully.

Cathy Caswell, Logosynthesis Practitioner (Canada)
Author, *Logosynthesis: Enjoying Life More Fully*

As a Core Coach, I found this book a powerful lantern: Hold it up in front of your eyes, and it will help you see where you are blocked on the path of abundance. With stories, testimonies, and thought-provoking exercises, Laurie and Willem invite you to heal your relationship with money while navigating through your core issues in a simple and easy way. Get ready to shift your mindset at its core in a snap.

Alan Rojas, Coach, CEO, Self (Peru)

If you really want to change your relationship with abundance this is THE BOOK. It helps you to deepen in a clear and simple way the theme of the scripts of life and to flush out the themes that condition you. It helps you to deepen. You can do the exercises as you read or take your time slowly. A book that becomes a traveling companion to abundance! Super recommended!

**Virna Trivellato, Logosynthesis Practitioner,
Energy Coach (Italy)**

Embrace Prosperity: Resolve Blocks to Experiencing Abundance is a book that has inspired me to look at any abundance issues in an entirely different manner. I find myself asking the question, what is in the way energetically and blocking my abundance? A wonderful easy and quick read that has potential for great returns.

**Judy Sabah, MCC, Certified Axiogenics© Coach,
Professional Speaker, Author (US)**

Embrace Prosperity has a very clear and engaging writing style and is rich in examples of applications of Logosynthesis. Another great tool from Willem and Laurie.

**Julie Jacinthe Arsenault, MSW Clinical Social Worker,
Psychotherapist, Logosynthesis Practitioner (Canada)**

Disclaimer

The authors and publisher of this material have used their best efforts in preparing this book. The authors and publisher make no representation or warranties with respect to the accuracy, applicability, fitness, or completeness of the contents of this book. They disclaim any warranties (expressed or implied), merchantability, or fitness for any particular purpose. The authors and publisher shall in no event be held liable for any loss or other damages, including but not limited to special, incidental, consequential, or other damages. As always, the advice of a competent legal, medical, accounting or other professional should be sought. This manual contains material protected under International and Federal Copyright Laws and Treaties. Any unauthorized reprint or use of this material is prohibited.

Free Tool

DOWNLOAD THIS NOW

You Will Need It

As you read this book you will find 3 important sentences used repeatedly.

Photograph these sentences (which you can find formatted at the end of this Special Report) and save them on your phone. Keep them close by so they will always be easy to find and use!

Just go to **www.BooksbyLaurie.com/guide**, and complete the form so we know where to send your download link and follow up tips. The download instructions for your personal copy of the *Quick Start Guide: Using Logosynthesis to Release Anxiety, Stress and Worry* will arrive by return email.

Contents

Advanced Praise 1
Free Tool 11
Chapter 1: Do You Believe in Scarcity? 15
Chapter 2: Getting Stuck in Scarcity 27
Chapter 3: Releasing Frozen Energy with Logosynthesis ... 41
Chapter 4: The Journey to Experiencing Abundance 55
Chapter 5: Discovering Your Own Path 77
Chapter 6: How Much is Enough Now? 93
Chapter 7: Challenges: Beyond Not Enough and Too
    Much 109
Chapter 8: The Mystery of Money 127
Chapter 9: The Mastery of Money — An Introduction .. 143
We Need Your Help 163
Logosynthesis Resources 165
Acknowledgements 169
About the Authors Dr. Laurie Weiss 173
How to Work with Dr. Laurie Weiss 175
About the Authors Dr. Willem Lammers 179
How to Work with Dr. Willem Lammers 181
Other Books by Dr. Laurie Weiss 183
Other Books by Dr. Willem Lammers 187

CHAPTER 1

DO YOU BELIEVE IN SCARCITY?

Have you ever been so terrified that you simply couldn't bring yourself to make an important financial decision? Do you have visions of being destitute? Meet Carolyn.

> **Carolyn** was stuck!
> She wanted to retire but was terrified that she would not have enough money to last her the rest of her life.

This is a common enough problem, but with one exception. Carolyn, an outstanding and respected professional woman, was a multimillionaire.

Logically, she knew that income from her investments could easily support her lifestyle without her ever having to spend the money she had been saving and investing for years. But logic didn't help—she still imagined being too poor to afford food.

As we talked about why she was so scared, she described memories from an impoverished childhood. She had been earning her own spending money before she was 10 years old. Then she said something startling, "When I put money in the bank, I still think it disappears forever."

Carolyn's parents insisted that she give them almost all her earnings to put into her bank account. She dutifully followed their rules but when she went to withdraw the money for a school trip, she discovered that the bank account was almost empty. Betrayed and furious that her parents had spent her hard-earned money, she vowed to never forgive them—and 50 years later she was still angry.

She had been overwhelmed by this experience of betrayal when she was 15 years old and could do nothing to change the situation. The situation was so painful that she effectively froze her energy to protect herself from the pain she felt. Instead, she focused her life around accumulating money. Yet the memory of her money in the bank disappearing stayed active enough to resurface 50 years later.

Life energy either enlivens you as it flows, or it blocks you if it doesn't. It is in the right place or the wrong place. Carolyn's energy not only wasn't flowing, but she had left some of it locked in a memory for 50 years. In the midst of material wealth, she had never experienced having enough. She not only believed in scarcity; she was stuck in scarcity.

Are You Stuck Too?

If you believe "I don't have enough" or "There isn't enough"—whether that's enough money, enough time, enough love, enough friends, or enough resources to do what you want to do in any area—then the answer is yes.

Laurie: I have been there. I once needed to make a daily choice between buying the lunch drink I wanted and the one I could afford. The difference in price was only two cents. This happened a long time ago, but the difference was very real to me when my personal spending budget was only five dollars a week.

Willem: I have been there, too. When I was 14 years old, my family was poor. One of my shoes had a hole in the toecap, because I had worn them for a long time. Because they were my only pair, I couldn't bring them to the shoemaker's shop to have them repaired. It took my parents weeks to collect the money for new shoes. In that time, I learned that there wasn't enough.

After many years of struggle, we learned a process that helped us release the last vestiges of those struggles and discover the abundance that truly exists in our worlds.

This book will help you discover and experience abundance in your relationship to money. But it just might overlap into those other areas, too.

You Need to Start Where You Are Now

If you don't feel like you have enough money, you've probably learned to believe some ideas like these:

- *Money burns a hole in your pocket*
- *The rich get richer and the poor get poorer*
- *You can't win for losing*
- *Money is the root of all evil*

- *One way to lose a friend is to lend him money*
- *Save it for a rainy day*
- *Marry a rich man—or woman*
- *Money doesn't grow on trees*
- *You spend money like it's going out of style*
- *We can't afford this*
- *It's only money*

Did you hear your parents, grandparents or religious institutions insist that this is the truth, even the absolute truth? How did hearing them help you learn to believe in scarcity?

Laurie: Whenever I teach a class about relieving money anxiety, the first thing I ask participants to do is create posters of statements they heard about money when they were children. We put them on the wall and refer to the statements throughout the workshop. Later, we try to answer the following questions about each statement:

- How did you learn this?
- Why did people in your environment repeat this when you were a child?
- How has this idea been useful to you in your life so far?
- Is the statement useful now?

Laurie lives and works in the US. Willem lives in Switzerland and works internationally. When we asked an international group of folks what they heard about money when they were children, these are some of the things they posted on the virtual wall of the Internet.

- *Money doesn't make happiness*
- *Learn to live within what money you earn or receive*
- *Don't throw away your old shoes before you get new ones*
- *Easy come, easy go*
- *Money doesn't grow on my back*

- *Money is not everything*
- *Money is all you need*
- *I'm not your ATM, I'm your parent*
- *Spend half, save half*
- *You will become a pauper*
- *It's too expensive*
- *You can only become rich by being a criminal*
- *You have to work hard for your money*

These messages are rarely shared with evil intent. Children don't experience limits and often share freely. Many people who grew up in poverty had no idea that they were poor when they were small. Others who grew up in wealthy families learned to fear not having enough.

Scarcity Is A Belief System

Most parents do their best to prepare their children for the world as they know it. Some parents do this from their own belief that there isn't enough, hoping to protect their children from what they believe to be the harsh realities of the world.

Almost everyone who is attracted to information about abundance has a childhood history of hearing statements like those we have listed. But not everyone believes that money is scarce.

Laurie: I once listened to one of my wealthy clients in wonder as he explained to me how his parents had routinely taught him about how to acquire and manage money in the world. He was a philanthropist and concerned with using his money to make the world a better place. For him, money was abundant, but love was scarce—which is why he was a client in the first place.

Fortunate people who believe in abundance and have enough money to be comfortable with it are rarely attracted to this kind of book. They either heard different, more useful, messages about money as children, or they have already examined and changed their old limiting beliefs.

What This Book is For

If you are reading this, you were probably exposed to limiting beliefs that taught you that there isn't enough money. In many cases, there were not enough other things as well, and you learned that many resources were scarce. The information about what to do about those scarce resources is extremely varied.

We do live in a world of limited resources, and the amount of money you earn or receive in other ways may be beyond your control. However, the fact that you're reading this book probably means more about how you think about having enough than how much you actually have in your bank account.

Reading this book will not immediately change the amount of money in your day to day life. *It is designed to help you resolve your limiting beliefs about scarcity and discover how to experience abundance instead.*

Money is the measure you probably use when you think about abundance or scarcity. It's not the only measure. It's often a stand-in for love, time, food, energy or other important commodities. Some people measure abundance by the number of toys they collect. Others do it by the number of people they can help.

You are unique, and your experience of the world is unique. That experience depends a lot on what you learned to pay attention to when you were a child. It also depends on how you were taught to manage the ongoing challenges of deciding how you use your resources.

In families that focus on scarcity, there is often a lack of information or a reluctance to use available information about how to manage those challenges. Because of that, they experience repeated cycles of scarcity that demand all the available energy to survive.

Practicing Abundance

You will be offered activities to help you learn to experience abundance in each chapter of this book. We suggest that you record your notes about each activity in a notebook or folder devoted to this work.

To get started, complete these sentences by filling in the blanks.

I currently experience scarcity around _____
(money, time, love…)

Three things I learned about this from important people in my life when I was a child are _____

By reading this book, I hope I will _____

Chapter 2

Getting Stuck in Scarcity

When you believe in scarcity you often feel compelled to do things to make sure that nothing challenges your comfortable beliefs. You may even sabotage your wealth, your work, your relationships and your health by making choices that are not in your best interest. You don't do what you know how to do, or you keep doing something that causes problems.

Carolyn kept working hard to earn money she didn't need, even though she wanted to retire, and her rational mind knew she had enough to be comfortable for the rest of her life.

Elaine's income had dropped drastically. In a money workshop she admitted that she had not changed her strategy for attracting clients in years, even though it no longer worked.

What's the Difference between Imagination and Reality?

Laurie: In 1984, my ignorance about scarcity and abundance nearly cost me my marriage and my business. My husband and I had been working together for about 12 years when we stumbled into producing a workshop taught by a money guru.

After several years of excitement and overwork I recognized that something was wrong. The numbers didn't work—and they really didn't. The workshop we were working so hard to produce was NOT making money. It was being subsidized by my other hard work.

I complained and was told I had a bad attitude. I did. I was viewing the situation from a valid perspective of scarcity of resources AND a belief system, a fantasy, that stopped me from seeing beyond that limiting perspective.

I "just knew" that I was right to stop supporting the workshop, and reached my conclusion based on that certainty rather than seeking other options.

Fast Forward Seven Years

In 2001, after I had spent much of the previous decade trying to make sense of my own relationship to money and abundance, I sent this email to other members of the fledging professional coaching community.

Financial sabotage

I am interested in exploring how to help people be more responsible about money issues in their lives. Often, they know what to do to take better care of themselves financially, but do not act on their information. I am currently collecting stories about how people sabotage their financial lives. If you have a story, or even a one liner, will you share it with me?

Responses poured in. One of the first I read started, "As a recovering scarcity expert, I have some thoughts for you! Is this for your clients, or research, even future project like a book? Just curious...." Looking back, I know the answer was yes on all counts.

Other responses reinforced my own views that this was a life pattern, developed early, that required much time and effort to change.

Fast forward to 2010 when I encountered a process that helped me understand that viewing everything in the world in terms of energy allowed these changes to happen astonishingly quickly: Logosynthesis.

Logosynthesis is a system for self-coaching and guided change. It was developed from energy psychology and other modalities by my co-author, Dr. Willem Lammers and offers a new and different way to help you discover the abundance that exists in your world.

In 2001, when I was exploring money and financial issues, Willem was searching for easier and more direct ways to serve clients when he discovered Logosynthesis in 2005. When we met in one of his workshops in 2011, I was incredibly impressed.

As Willem continued to develop new applications of Logosynthesis, I continued attending his programs and eventually used my skills as a writer to translate his work into an introductory book for the general public.

When Willem first applied Logosynthesis to money, I eagerly learned his framework and combined it with my own work on the subject. When I asked about participating in the new, online version of his work on Logosynthesis and abundance and described why I was interested, he suggested that we collaborate in writing this book.

Willem: I came from a background of scarcity, in which everybody always worked hard to pay the bills, and that's what I've done. After I became self-employed, I founded two training institutes and ran them for more than 30 years.

After I sold my last institute, I kept working hard, as if the scarcity still existed, even though my business had done well enough to guarantee me a good pension. It took me several years to realize how exhausting that was.

I discovered how deep this pattern was rooted when I was developing new Logosynthesis workshops on relationships, health, and money. I realized how the idea of scarcity kept me going when it wasn't necessary anymore.

Bandwidth and Energy

Others have been exploring the same question in very different ways.

Research shows that our mental resources, known as our bandwidth, are limited, and when these resources are low, so is our self-control. We then respond more emotionally and less logically than we would when we are fresh and ready to go. Each task that takes some of our mental resources or energy makes us less likely to respond logically to our next task.

Spiritually, the energy of the universe is boundless, and it flows through each of us. As human beings, we have the potential to experience this boundless energy, this Essence. However, we exist in biological bodies that must be nourished and nurtured in order to tap into this boundless energy.

That is where bandwidth comes in. We have a limited amount of biological energy which supports our psychological well-being and mental capacity to allow us to experience that boundless spiritual energy.

The new science of behavioral economics works with the concept of mental and psychological bandwidth. The authors of *Scarcity: Why Having Too Little Means So Much*, Edgar Shafir, Ph.D. and Sendhil Mullainathan, Ph.D., explored the question of why poor people continually make poor decisions about their financial lives.

They concluded that when you (referring to people in general) feel you lack something, your mind works less efficiently. You tend to focus intensely on solving your most pressing problems—a process called tunneling. You lack enough energy to imagine the future and to take action to avoid later problems. It is hard to do anything besides taking care of yourself in the moment.

Finding New Options

We, Carolyn, Laurie and Willem, all concluded that we lacked money—for entirely different reasons. But the effect was quite similar. None of us could solve our respective problems without finding some additional energy.

Carolyn's energy was frozen in her childhood pain of discovering that her money was missing. When we eventually released that energy, her life changed almost immediately. Later, you'll learn how she reclaimed her energy and how you can reclaim yours also.

Laurie's energy came from dropping her involvement in the workshop. That story and its relationship to codependency is told in her book, *What Is the Emperor Wearing? Truth-Telling in Business Relationships.*

For Willem, the development of Logosynthesis created ways to let go of the scarcity patterns that had existed for most of his life, and to become aware of his freedom to live as he had always desired. His books explain many different ways to free your energy.

Everything is Energy

But what is energy anyway? If you took science classes in school, you learned about different forms of energy, like heat, electricity and magnetism. Now we focus on energy from fossil fuels vs. renewable energy sources.

Ancient Chinese philosophers described human energy as ch'i. In India, it is called prana, in Egypt, Ka, and in Western philosophy, *élan vital*. There are many other names and there seems to be universal agreement that if this energy is to be useful it must be free to move.

Spiritual traditions also agree that there is a universal energy source, with names ranging from the many names of God to simply Oneness. Willem uses the word Essence to describe this energy.

Getting stuck in anything usually implies a lack of movement or natural flow. When your life energy flows freely and naturally, you move from one activity to another with minimal stress and maximum pleasure. When your life energy isn't moving, a part of you feels stuck or frozen.

Part of your energy (the Real Self) is in flow while other parts freeze because they are adapting or rebelling in response to outside pressures. The problem is that we have lots of frozen parts which not only don't cooperate, but also sometimes even sabotage each other.

When a part of you believes the messages about scarcity you heard as a child, some of your life energy gets stuck in that part, too. When you are surrounded by others who also experience limited resources in their lives, you learn to believe what they believe—after all you see, hear and experience evidence of these beliefs regularly.

This happened for Carolyn when she learned that the money she thought her parents had saved for her had been spent because they "needed it." This was one of many different ways her parents let her know that resources were scarce and that she should never expect to have enough.

You can only experience abundance when your energy is flowing. This book is designed to help you change your experience of scarcity to an experience of abundance as you release the energy bound up in those limiting beliefs.

Words Affect Energy

As psychotherapists, we have both been using words to help people release stuck or frozen energy for many years. However, we were awed when we encountered the incredible power of using the words Willem discovered to rapidly facilitate those changes.

You can read the story of Willem's discovery of Logosynthesis in his book, *Self Coaching With Logosynthesis*. His English language book for professionals is *Logosynthesis: Healing with Words: A Handbook for the Helping Professions.*

Laurie describes her first experiences with these words in *Letting It Go: Relieve Anxiety and Toxic Stress in Just a Few Minutes Using Only Words (Rapid Relief with Logosynthesis®)*. That book is an excellent introduction to this material and is available wherever books are sold.

We have each written many other books you'll find listed in the resource section of this book.

This powerful system that we describe in the next chapter is the key to unlocking the energy that is frozen in those outmoded beliefs and releasing it to help you experience joy and abundance in your life now.

Practicing Abundance

How has your financial awareness grown and changed throughout your life? Is it moving in the right direction for you?

Where is your energy flowing and your life working well? Where does your energy seem to be stuck?

Do you have enough bandwidth to manage your financial life now? If not, where do you suspect you can find the energy you need to experience financial abundance?

You may not be clear about all the answers to these questions right now. Record your thoughts and keep reading as we explain how much easier it is to reclaim your stuck energy than you might imagine.

Chapter 3

Releasing Frozen Energy with Logosynthesis

"Before I learned about Logosynthesis, I believed that thoughts about money are true or false. Now I know that all thoughts are just thoughts. They come and go and are not solid and they can be changed."—A workshop participant

Frozen Energy Leaves Clues

What conversation are you afraid to have?

- Helen didn't want to talk about how she was going to pay her share of the rent after she lost her job.
- Max avoided telling his best friend that he couldn't afford to be the best man at his friend's destination wedding.
- Elyse changed the subject whenever her husband asked her if she had talked to her boss about getting the raise that they both knew she deserved.

What task do you keep putting off?

- Leonard wouldn't open his mail. He just piled it on a corner of the table. When the pile fell over, he stuffed it into a drawer.
- Dr. Ted couldn't bring himself to dictate the client notes he needed to bill the insurance company for his services.

- Jennifer kept putting off making reservations for a show she wanted to see. By the time she got to it, the show was sold out.

There's a reason that each person avoided doing these useful activities. You may think that what isn't being done is the problem, *but it's really a little more complicated than that.*

Simply by learning to live in this world, you experienced situations that overwhelmed you. When this happened, some of your energy froze around that experience and left a tiny part of you behind as you continued to grow and change.

These left-behind parts have agendas of their own. The reason one part (B) may be blocking another part (A) is because B imagines that doing what A suggests will cause you to feel the distress you felt when you were unable to manage a similar problem in your past.

It is in those images of the past or fantasies of the future where your energy is frozen. Finding and releasing that blocked energy and letting it flow so you can use it in your life is what the Logosynthesis process is about.

Logosynthesis is Simple and Profound

This process is based on a few simple ideas and is implemented by saying three simple sentences.

The ideas are:

- Everything is energy.
- Energy is either flowing or it's stuck.
- Energy either belongs to you, or it doesn't.
- Words get stuck energy moving.

Jennifer experienced saying three simple sentences that allowed her to experience her world in a whole new way.

First, she examined what happened each time she thought about purchasing the tickets. She imagined booking online, going through the steps of entering her name and credit card number. Then she identified a physical reaction to the memory, a tight feeling in her shoulders, each time she started toward the computer. As soon as she got distracted by something else, the tightness disappeared.

A workshop partner read these sentences to her a phrase at a time and she repeated them. Her partner paused after each sentence to allow time for her to notice how the words impacted her thoughts, feelings and experiences.

> 1. *I retrieve all my energy bound up in this image of the computer screen and all that it represents and take it to the right place in myself.*

Pause

> 2. *I remove all non-me energy related to this image of the computer screen and all that it represents, from all of my cells, my body and my personal space, and send it to where it truly belongs.*

Pause.

3. I retrieve all my energy bound up in all my reactions to this image of the computer screen and all that it represents and take it to the right place in myself.

Pause.

When she completed the process, she was smiling. She said, "I remember my Mom refusing to let me go to the movies with my friends because I hadn't done my chores. I am in charge now and I know that I will always have something left on my list to complete. That's no reason to stop myself from having fun."

The image of Jennifer's computer screen had activated a hidden, distressing memory of Jennifer's past, which had kept her from booking a ticket. The Logosynthesis sentences resolved that frozen memory and freed her life energy.

I was happy to get an email from her a few weeks later in which she told me how much she had enjoyed the show.

This is often how Logosynthesis works as a tool to get your life energy moving again. You can learn to use the sentences from books and classes that are easily available. More are being developed by many professionals working in the fields of psychotherapy, counseling, coaching and education.

Logosynthesis Offers Much More

You can get current information by joining one of the several Facebook Logosynthesis groups. The two books Willem recommends to begin your journey are first my book, *Letting It Go: Relieve Anxiety and Toxic Stress in Just a Few Minutes Using Only Words (Rapid Relief with Logosynthesis®)* and second, his book, *Self-Coaching With Logosynthesis: How the power of words can change your life.*

You'll find these and other references in the resource section of this book.

You will find references to other materials, as well. Logosynthesis was first developed as a process that professionals could use to help their clients rapidly resolve issues of trauma, anxiety, depression and other serious problems.

If you discover that you have frozen energy around serious issues such as these, we strongly recommend that you seek professional help instead of trying to resolve them yourself.

The Logosynthesis International Association has developed a certification process to help you identify qualified resources.

Using the Words
Your challenge will be to follow the simple instructions we offer to find the images or sounds that represent hid-

den memories, beliefs or fantasies. When you have uncovered this information, you can use it to construct your own sentences.

You have probably avoided thinking about those memories, beliefs and fantasies because you are afraid they will reactivate the pain that overwhelmed you in the past or that you expect to feel again in the future.

Once that was necessary, but it's not needed anymore. With the help of the Logosynthesis sentences you can let go of the pain in a way that's far easier and less stressful than you ever imagined it could be. It may even be fun.

The sentences below each have a blank space to be filled in with words describing something that represents your frozen energy. This is where you start.

1. I retrieve all my energy bound up in _____ and take it to the right place in myself.

> 2. *I remove all non-me energy related to _____ from all of my cells, my body and my personal space and send it to where it truly belongs.*
> 3. *I retrieve my energy bound up in all my reactions to _____ and take it to the right place in myself.*

Once you have discovered where your energy is stuck, you can complete each sentence by filling in the blank with a brief description of whatever represents the stuck energy.

When you are learning to use this process for yourself, it is a good idea to write out each sentence before you start to read them aloud. Remember to pause for at least 30 seconds after saying each sentence. This allows time for the words to do their work.

Of course, having a partner read you the words a few at a time is even easier. Either way is fine.

A logical part in you may be trying to make sense of these words and figure out 'the right place.' If that happens, trust the process: You don't need to know. Just relax and experiment anyhow.

As you read further, you'll find more information and tips about using this process. *Letting It Go* has a very detailed description. If you haven't downloaded your free tool yet, do it now at **www.BooksbyLaurie.com/guide**.

The worst thing that can happen when you practice this is nothing. You can't hurt yourself. Many people have found the process life-changing.

Even we as professionals can't predict what will happen using the sentences with our clients, but we all share the experience that the sentences tend to help people. Relax and simply notice what does happen and keep practicing.

Practicing Abundance

A good way to find out where your energy is frozen is to create a list of 10 or 100 things you would like to be, do and/or have in your life. This list can include major things like your 'bucket list' of things you want to do before you die. It can also include simple things like having a clear desk, organized closet or special meal.

Do this quickly. It doesn't need to take longer than 30 minutes.

(We disagree a bit about this process, so you can choose your own number. Willem believes this exercise needs a list of only 10 items while Laurie thinks a list of 100 items is more valuable. Try it each way if you like, and let us know what works for you.)

First, take some lined paper and number each line from 1 to 10 or 1 to 100. Sit down and write as fast as you can, one item on a line without thinking about it very much.

It's okay if you repeat yourself—that just means the item is particularly important to you.

Now study your list carefully. Observe and make notes of your own thoughts: Why is it difficult for you to have this? Each of these thoughts may represent a place where energy is stuck.

You may also explore how you've been procrastinating in your financial life. We are focusing on finances here, but it could be in any other area of your life, as well.

CHAPTER 4

THE JOURNEY TO EXPERIENCING ABUNDANCE

Making the transition from believing in scarcity to experiencing abundance is the result of a shift in your energy system. You will release the energy you have locked into old beliefs, and that will allow you to recognize new possibilities in your current situation.

Logosynthesis often releases the barriers to creating a change in your financial life. The facts may be impossible to change because of a social or political situation beyond your control, but you can always develop a new perspective on your world.

Where Do You Start?

If you are just starting on this journey and your basic needs for food and shelter and medical care are managed, you may still

- struggle to pay your bills
- secretly blame others for your financial situation
- think you're not getting paid as much as you deserve
- admire rich people
- wonder why other people seem to have so much more money than you do
- spend all your money when you intended to build up your saving reserve

- feel like you can't even keep up, let alone get ahead financially
- worry about money

Your choices are probably based on whatever grabs your attention at the moment. The world is filled with distractions. Your phone and tablet offer an overwhelming stream of suggestions about how to spend your time and your money.

Movies, media and advertising show you endless possibilities of how famous people live their lives, implying that you should follow their example. If you can't do these things, you may conclude that the problem is in you. It isn't!

Important Stepping Stones

An important part of this journey is shifting your focus from what goes on around you to an entirely different space. A space where the questions are different. You become more aware of a different reality—of Essence. Now you wonder:

- *Who am I really?*
- *Why am I here?*
- *Who are all these other people?*
- *How are we connected?*
- *What is my unique contribution to all this?*

This is a gradual change. Some shifts happen in an instant, but they are stepping stones. This journey doesn't happen over days or weeks—some steps take years. What we offer here is some help along your way.

Tools You Can Use

Remember your list of 10 or 100 things you would like to be, do or have in your life? Writing it quickly was a way to move beyond your surface awareness and instead toward answers to some of the questions listed above.

Review the list and, if you chose the list of 100, pay special attention to the last 20 or 30 items you listed. You may find clues there to your most important priorities—maybe even to your life's true work.

Knowing your life mission or your life's true work guides the choices you make to allow you to experience abundance.

Laurie: Many years before I was clear about answers to these important questions, I discovered a simple shorthand question that I still use to guide my choices. The question is "Is this a beckon or a hum?"

This is a quick way to answer two important questions.

1. Do I want this thing only because of outside stimulation? I experience this kind of stimulation like sweets *beckoning* to me from a bakery window and inviting me to eat them.
2. Does my desire for this thing arise from within me? Is this like a background *hum* that is hard to ignore?

I often feel pulled to respond to the outside stimulation because it acts as a trigger to a past experience of pleasure.

I've discovered that the kind of pleasure I get from saying yes to the *beckon* does not last long and sometimes interferes with honoring my long-term goals. That is why I hide my chocolate and other sweets in cabinets where I don't accidentally encounter them.

On the other hand, if I respond to the *hum* that arises spontaneously, I usually feel very satisfied. I take those sweets out of the cabinet when a hum for them arises—and I enjoy them and experience enough quite quickly.

This is one way that I experience abundance. I learned it originally as a weight control method, and it has been very effective in helping me discern how much is enough for me in many different situations.

Experiment with answering those questions, either with or without the shortcut.

Our Journeys
As co-authors of this book, living on two different continents, with vastly different life experiences, we find it

useful to share how we each traveled our own very different life paths from experiencing scarcity to experiencing abundance. On this path, the journey is as important and exciting as the destination.

Our destinations are very similar. We both experience abundance every day. We each enjoy enough money to live comfortably and do things that please us. We each experience the love and support of family, friends and our professional communities. Neither of us needs to work to earn money anymore. Instead, our money works for us.

We each came to our own methods of teaching others about experiencing abundance. Our paths converged when a mutual colleague invited me, Laurie, to study the system of guided life change, Logosynthesis, that Willem had developed. One of the reasons I accepted the unusual premises of this new system was that it worked. But another is that Willem and I both had earned our teaching certifications from the International Transactional Analysis Association.

When Willem first developed a workshop called *Coins* that used Logosynthesis to release frozen energy that kept people from using money effectively in their lives, I was excited about learning his methods. It all meshed beautifully with what I had been teaching for a long time. When I expressed interest in watching Willem teach his new workshop about money on the Internet, he suggested that we write this book together.

Laurie's Journey

I can still remember my days as a young, newly-married, recent college graduate who had to make a careful decision about every penny I spent. So much has changed since then, and I am grateful for all that has happened that has made those changes possible.

I'm one of a small percentage of people my age in the United States who is comfortably retired after a thoroughly satisfying and fulfilling career as a psychotherapist, consultant and coach. However, I haven't retired from my life mission of helping others emerge from the boxes their families and cultures taught them to live in. I carry out my mission now through writing and publishing books to help individuals experience joy and abundance in their lives and relationships.

It wasn't always this way. Although I was raised in a middle-class family and I've always had more than enough material things, I was taught to believe in scarcity. And no wonder—my parents met and married in New York City during the Great Depression of the 1930s. They must have experienced scarcity wherever they looked.

Once, when I realized that my mother had started working in her father's grocery store when she was about eight years old, I commented on it, and she told me, "All immigrant families worked." I was startled when I realized that although both my parents were born in the US, all their parents immigrated from Russia and Eastern Europe in the early years of the 20th century. I had never before thought of them growing up as members of immigrant families.

I was taught to believe in scarcity and to save what I earned for important goals, like going to college or buying a house. I was taught to carefully conserve my resources. None of that advice was bad, and following it has served me well.

The part that hasn't served me was the built-in definition that *there wasn't and wouldn't be enough*. I could never really relax and enjoy what I did have because of the fear and constraint that went with that belief.

It's been a lifelong journey move from "earn, save, spend only on necessities" to "earn, save, spend, invest, enjoy and share." This journey also included learning to work and share with a life partner who urged me to do what I considered to be irresponsible things with money.

There been many bumps in the road since we married in 1960. Overall, it's been both fun as well as challenging.

My first awareness of the need for financial literacy beyond knowing how to balance my checkbook came in 1976 when my husband and I were blamed for competition problems and excluded from a group practice we'd started with professional colleagues several years earlier. This painful experience was largely the result of ignorance and the mismanagement of the financial aspects of our business.

Continuing our practice and teaching on our own made us squarely responsible for the financial success of our business. We needed help so we started out on our financial and management education.

A casual conversation with another colleague some years later led to the question, "If we're so smart how come we're not rich?" Our colleague invited us to a workshop about money that opened the door to two very different things. One was a focus on important practical aspects of creating wealth beyond just what you could earn. The other was a beginning awareness of the energy aspects of money.

Our journey included a deliberate education about how money works in the world. It included books and workshops about the practical, the metaphysical and the spiritual energy of money. Willem and I will share some of these tools throughout his book as we encourage you to begin or continue your own journey to experience abundance.

A small inheritance from my husband's parents allowed us to make a larger down payment on a home a little bit earlier than we had planned. A small inheritance from my parents made almost no difference in our lives.

Our journey also included some major mistakes including a money-losing attempt at investing in real estate. In that case, doing something we did not love doing, in an effort to create wealth, led us badly off course.

I learned to enjoy both the process and the rewards of creating the experience of abundance in our lives. This money has arrived in our lives because we focused our energy on our important life work: helping others get what was most important to them.

Now the financial abundance in our lives comes from income from investing some of the money we earned while doing that life work. Those investments were suggested by our financial advisors.

Even now I sometimes pinch myself when I spend what used to be an unthinkably large sum of money. I remind myself that there is enough. Now, my biggest challenge is finding the time to balance doing all my projects with all the wonderful possibilities for relaxation and play that I also enjoy.

I still use the question, "Is this a beckon or a hum?" to guide my decisions.

Willem's Journey

I come from a family with scarce resources, and limitations were built in my belief system very early: *There is not enough, and it's not o.k. if you want more than we have.*

There was also a belief that the rich were "other" people, while we belonged to the poor. There was also another, very important belief: I learned that it was possible to change my situation. If we as kids worked hard, we could climb up the ladder.

These beliefs were not invented by my parents: they were very usual in Western Europe in the 50's and 60's. WWII had left enormous damage, the Netherlands had to be rebuilt and this was perceived as a common effort. Scarcity was a matter of fact, but there was also the trust that progress was possible.

There were contradictory beliefs about education: Some parents thought it was important that children earned money as soon as they were able to. Others believed in the value of higher education. My parents belonged to the latter group.

From an early age, I learned that money should be spent on things that are necessary or useful. Spending money just for fun, taking risks or even gambling, was a no-go.

My family didn't invest in the stock market, only in bonds, and even now, I don't understand much about investing money. However, it was very clear that every family should own a house, and a mortgage should be paid off. I remember being surprised when a friend of mine told me that someone came to his house to pick up the rent: I didn't know what that was.

When Luzia and I bought real estate, we managed to amortize a great part in a short time. We also took care to save for a good pension, in the same way my parents had done, and we didn't make big trips or buy a new car until it was clear that we'd be financially safe later in life.

Only after the recipes of my family of origin had allowed me to create a certain financial stability did I learn that money is my servant and not my boss. After a long period of scarcity, first on the level of daily experience, later only in my head, I discovered that money was just energy. I vividly remember the Logosynthesis session in which I discovered this.

A client had a conflict about money with some family members, and I used a mapping technique, in which the client places markers for the people involved in different places in the room.

Then the client is invited to take the place of other people and objects to explore what they become aware of while standing on those spots.

Because in this session money was such an important issue, I decided to create a marker for that, too.

To my surprise, when the client stood on the money marker, nothing happened. Taking the role of the money, the client felt somewhat dull, completely neutral, indifferent to all the meanings it got from the people around it. The money had no value or meaning by itself.

At this moment I discovered that it's up to me to decide what money means to me, and I started to leave behind what I had learned about it in my childhood.

From the moment I knew that money was just energy. I could decide what form that energy could take: buy objects, attend training, travel or give it away. I could choose between a long-distance trip, a car, new furniture, helping people after a disaster or leaving it in my savings account for later use.

Before that moment, it was "allowed" for me to spend money on computer equipment and professional training. It took many years before my wife and I decided to go to Mexico, New Zealand or Cambodia, just for the joy of traveling.

At 60, I bought my first new car, in the right color, with all the gimmicks and gadgets I liked, without any further justification.

I finally learned that abundance is there wherever you look, and that money for fun is sometimes well-invested.

What Comes Next

Practical aspects of creating wealth, the money you get to keep rather than spend, are available from many different sources. These aspects are important to learn, but hard to use when your energy is frozen in ways that prevent you from noticing they exist or considering putting them into practice.

The purpose of this book is to help you release your own energy that's blocking your experience of abundance, therefore, we'll offer you exercises. By the time you have finished them, you'll easily learn those practical aspects of creating wealth, and we will suggest resources to help you do so.

Practicing Abundance

Taking ideas and putting them into action is a challenge for many. It is almost as if there is an energy barrier to be crossed.

First you need to discover your own personal energy barrier. Do this by finding a trigger, an image or a voice that interferes with you doing what you want to do. One way to do this is to sit quietly and think about times that this has happened. Notice any image or voice associated with this memory.

Another way is to notice what you think about when you are considering spending money on a specific item. You may hear a voice from the space around you, scolding you or warning you to be cautious. Or you may create a conversation with an imagined critic while balancing your checkbook or thinking of asking for a raise.

The variety of different voices and images you encounter depends upon your own personal history.

Such an image or a voice is a trigger for distress. It can be neutralized with the help of the Logosynthesis sentences.

Once you have found an image or a voice, repeat the following sentences aloud to help you get past this energy barrier and actually do the suggested activities.

> 1. *I retrieve all my energy bound up in (this image or voice of X) and take it to the right place in my Self.*
>
> *Breathe and take time to notice any thoughts, feelings, sounds, images and sensations you experience.*

THE JOURNEY TO EXPERIENCING ABUNDANCE 75

2. I remove all non-me energy related to (this image or voice of X) from all of my cells, my body and my personal space and send it to where it truly belongs.

Breathe and take time to notice any thoughts, emotions, sounds, images and sensations you experience.

3. I retrieve my energy bound up in all my reactions to (this image or voice of X) and take it to the right place in my Self.

Breathe and take time to notice any thoughts, feelings, sounds, images and sensations you experience.

Now notice what happened to the image or the voice. How does this free your energy to do what you want or need to do?

If your energy doesn't feel free yet, repeat the process. What other images or voices are showing up in the space around you? Repeat the three sentences for this new or changed image or voice.

This process can contain a number of steps; take one at a time. Lindsay, who had a secure income, noticed a voice while considering whether to purchase a new winter coat she could easily afford. "What if you don't earn enough money to pay for this?"

She used "this voice warning me about not earning enough money" in her first set of sentences. During this process she remembered a scene in which father angrily warned her mother not to spend money. She repeated the sentences using "this image of my parents arguing about money" as the trigger blocking her energy. Then she felt complete.

When you are ready to move on, say the fourth Logosynthesis sentence aloud:

4. I tune all of my systems to this new awareness.

CHAPTER 5

DISCOVERING YOUR OWN PATH

What keeps you from experiencing abundance in your financial life?

- Jerry was ashamed about his financial situation and knew that he wasn't allowed to talk about it.
- Betty believed you had to be born rich in order to have money.

- Mary Jane was certain the money couldn't buy happiness and decided she would rather be happy than rich.
- Robert believed that he could never earn enough money.
- Peter was convinced that he couldn't survive without a regular paycheck and had to stay in a job he hated rather than risk moving.

You can use the Logosynthesis sentences to dissolve those blocks. However, sometimes it's hard to figure out just what those blocks are. The more precisely you identify what triggers your beliefs in scarcity, the more likely you are to successfully release the energy stored in those beliefs.

Once you retrieve your own energy and remove the energy bound in the influence of others, you'll learn what abundance will mean to you.

Here are two different activities that will help you identify some of these personal blocks. The first is a personal journey, and the second one introduces ideas from people who experience financial abundance but which may be foreign to you.

You can finish reading this book and come back to these activities later, if you prefer. Remember though, if you want to release your energy to use it to truly experience abundance and relieve your anxiety about money issues, it is important to actually practice the activities. That way you will discover the hidden triggers in your field and release the energy that is stored in them.

The Timeline Experiment

The first, a Logosynthesis technique, allows you to create a map of certain aspects of your life. You're going to create a map that will take you from the present time to a state of experiencing abundance.

This technique is done best if you can walk through your physical space in a room, but if that's not possible, you can also use space on a desk or table.

Taking turns doing this activity with a friend is ideal, but doing it alone is also effective.

You need to start with your goal, a concrete target that you hope to achieve in the future. If you're not sure what your target might be, go back to your list of 10 or 100 things you would like to be, do or have, and choose something from that list. You'll also need some small objects or pieces of paper to use as markers.

Find a spot that represents where you are now in your life and place a marker on that spot.

1. Choose a spot that represents your goal. Place the goal marker some distance away from the spot that represents your current life position.
2. On the line between them start moving away from the present spot and toward your goal. (If you are doing this with a friend, have your friend walk with you and record your thoughts as you say them

aloud. If you are doing it alone, simply write out your thoughts or record them on your phone.

3. Move slowly, observe your thoughts and notice your physical reactions along the way. If you're working on a flat surface, let your finger trace the distance and follow the same instructions.

4. If a thought, an image, a voice or a physical sensation of a hindrance creates an obstacle between you and your goal, drop a marker at that spot and record your thought.

5. Say the sentence, "*I retrieve all my energy bound up in (your description of this obstacle) and take it back to the right place in my Self.*" Your friend who is recording the process can lead you through the sentence, or you can refer to what you have written and say it yourself.

6. Continue on the path and mark and respond to any other obstacles in the same way.

7. Once you've reached the marker of your target, explore if there are any blocks left in that spot. If yes,

resolve them with the Logosynthesis sentences. Then return to the marker for the present time.

8. Now walk the path again and notice if there are any obstacles left. If there are, stand on the spot you've marked, identify and explore the obstacle and say the Logosynthesis sentences you used in Chapters 3 and 4.

Affirmations Help Identify Triggers

Some spiritual traditions use affirmations, stating something as if it were true over and over again, in an attempt to change your belief system. While this process had some value when we knew energy was frozen and didn't have the technology, we can let it go now. The Logosynthesis sentences work much more quickly than the long tedious process of affirming the new belief. However, it's extremely useful to discover how you react to a different belief system than the one you have learned over a long period of time.

Here are some common beliefs (affirmations) that are held by people who experience abundance.

- *I deserve to be wealthy.*
- *Abundance is natural.*
- *Every dollar I circulate enriches the economy and comes back to me vastly multiplied.*
- *Part of all I earn is mine to keep.*
- *My financial worth increases every day, whether I'm working, sleeping, or playing.*
- *All my investments are profitable.*
- *A lot more money is flowing into my life.*
- *I deserve it and will use it for my good and that of others.*

How do you react when you read each of these statements? Don't be embarrassed or surprised if you are reacting very negatively. The first time I, Laurie, read them aloud, I couldn't imagine how any of them could be true.

Working with these sentences will help you discover areas in which your energy about experiencing financial abundance is frozen. They'll also uncover triggers you can insert into the Logosynthesis sentences to release this energy.

Take whichever sentence you react to most strongly and work with it this way. Reserve about half an hour for each practice session. Writing this out with a pen and paper engages more aspects of your brain and is more powerful and effective than doing it on a computer.

One way to do this is to divide your paper vertically in half and write one sentence from the above list once in one column. Pause and notice any physical, mental or emotional responses you have. Now describe your response in the second column. Starting each sentence in the second column with the words, "yes, but…" is often useful.

If you reacted most strongly to "I deserve to be wealthy," write this in the left column. In the right column write your reaction. It might be "yes, but I don't really" or "yes, but my shoulders feel tense" or "yes, but I feel sad."

Repeat the process. Write the sentence again, pause, notice your response, record your response. Continue to repeat this process until

1. you feel a sense of completion, or
2. you run out of time.

Each annoying or disturbing reaction represents a place where your energy is stuck.

Releasing Stuck Energy

Now it's time to experiment with releasing that stuck energy. One way to clear this energy is to repeat this process 24 hours later and again 24 hours after that, over and over again, until your negative reactions disappear.

A more gentle and elegant way to release the energy from this negative reaction is to use the Logosynthesis sentences.

Each reaction can lead you to a belief, an image or a repetitive voice that points towards frozen energy.

Your goal is to find the words to fill in the blank in each Logosynthesis sentence with a statement that describes the trigger.

"Yes, but's" and similar reactions are triggered by images or voices in your personal space.

- These images or voices can be *memories*: You saw someone or heard someone who looked or sounded in a certain way. Usually these are memories of important people like parents or teachers.
- These images or voices can also be *fantasies*: You create an imaginary video in which something painful or threatening will happen in the future or could have happened in the past. You can imagine that you will go bankrupt and will have to sleep under a bridge or you imagine what could

have happened if your parents hadn't given you money when you were broke.

- The images or voices can also be *beliefs*: A belief is a statement you can see, because it's written, or you can hear, because it's spoken. If you use a belief as a trigger you use the image of the written text or a voice that speaks the belief.

Use this format: *this image of* (a memory, fantasy or belief) _____ for your statement. You can also *this voice saying*_____ in your statement.

Avoid using emotions such as angry, scared or sad in the sentences. Emotions are reactions to triggering experiences. It's best to locate the memory, belief or fantasy that occurred just before the sadness emerged and use that in the sentences.

For example, sadness might have been triggered by a memory of a month when you did not have enough money to pay your rent on time. In that case, you might use "This memory of not having the money to pay the rent"

Once you have your statement, use it to complete these sentences.

Before you say the sentences, notice how strongly you react to this memory and rate it from 0-10.

1. *I retrieve all my energy bound up in _____ and take it to the right place in my Self.*
2. *I remove all non-me energy related to _____ from all of my cells, my body and my personal space and send it to where it truly belongs.*
3. *I retrieve all my energy bound up in all my reactions to _____ and take it to the right place in my Self.*

Now say the sentences to yourself or with a partner, remembering to pause and observe your responses after saying each one. When you're done, say the negative statement again and rate how strongly you still react to it. Notice whether the number has changed.

Usually the number goes down. If it doesn't, there are different options:

- Always explore whether there are changes in the images or voices you started with. One aspect of an event neutralized by the sentences can uncover another aspect of the same event, or even another memory.
- If you don't notice any changes, just repeat the sentences in the form you used before.
- If the memory has changed its form or if a new memory has shown up, say the sentences for this new form or this new memory.

A memory of the face of a teacher in school can turn into the voice of that teacher, but it can also change to the face of your father. Working with the sentences is not a question of applying them once, there are many memories, fantasies and beliefs to be neutralized.

Another Bonus Gift

If you would like more samples of triggers used to resolve issues around scarcity, money and related issues, you can download help here: **www.BooksbyLaurie.com/triggers**. These samples will help you formulate your own triggering phrases to use in the Logosynthesis® sentences. You can also find a list of 50 additional triggers in *Letting It Go*, Chapter 6.

Practicing Abundance

You may find that you are spontaneously making small changes in your life just as a result of starting to read this book and noticing your relationship to money. Here are some small changes others reported.

- Bea: *"I learned to balance my checkbook."*
- Dean: *"I kept track of all the money I spent for a week by writing the amount on a card each time I made a purchase."*
- Marie: *"I started putting my bills in a basket near the front door instead of in stacks all over my apartment."*
- Stephen: *"I started buying books in a used bookstore instead of ordering new ones online."*
- Juanita: *"I subscribed to a newsletter on money and I'm reading an article from it every day."*

If you start making small changes like this, be sure to acknowledge them and celebrate.

CHAPTER 6

HOW MUCH IS ENOUGH NOW?

Clearing the energy blocks to experiencing abundance isn't the same thing as experiencing abundance! It's the first of many steps on this journey.

You probably already know many of the things you can do to take care of yourself financially. However, your inner programming has been in the way and you have not done them.

Even when you release the emotional and psychological barriers to experiencing abundance in your life, you still have a lifetime of habits that support your experience of scarcity. You have very little idea of what abundance looks, feels, sounds, smells and tastes like.

The media you're exposed to gives you images to fill these gaps. But are they really images of abundance or are they images of opulence—overabundance? You may not even have any kind of internal measure of what "enough" means to you.

Discovering What's Right for You

Ideally, you should now be able to use your inner guidance system to help you find what satisfies you. However, that guidance system probably provides misinformation. It's inaccurate because it's like a compass next to a magnet. Family, cultural and advertising messages you've been exposed to are pulling it off course.

It's hard to know what's just right for you now. You did when you were small and complained bitterly when your environment was not just right for you, but since then you've been "civilized," programmed according to the expectations of people and the world around you.

Instead of paying attention to your internal awareness of "just right," you pay attention to what influential people in your life and the media have told or demonstrated to you about how much you should have.

Learn to Notice Your Own Behavior

When your energy is flowing freely you respond to your own biological and emotional signals in the moment. You feel hunger and fatigue as physical sensations. You get what you need, whether it is food, rest, contact with others or time alone to pursue your life's work.

Generally, when those signals arise again, you repeat the process. You are also aware of the needs of others and learn to modify your own flow to not interfere with theirs. Sometimes you choose to interrupt your own flow temporally but get back to it as soon as you can.

Sometimes though, you do things just because you have gotten into the habit of doing them. They might have started in response to a natural energy flow—like stopping for a cup of coffee when you were tired. The first time, you enjoyed the coffee and felt re-energized and went on about your day.

The next day, instead of stopping because you were tired, you saw the coffee shop, remembered the pleasant visit the day before, and stopped again. Soon you, like Anita, were stopping there every day and it no longer had any connection to your own energy flow. You barely noticed the activity.

Anita was surprised when she realized how much time and money she was using for a daily coffee break that had no real value to her. She recognized that she was responding to advertising (outside energy) that promoted the idea that she deserved a small luxury that would make her feel happy.

Once she realized that she was doing what was being programmed instead of noticing what her own energy prompted her to do, she decided to take a break only when she noticed that she really wanted to. She started enjoying her occasional coffee shop visits again.

It is worth noticing how many things you do are a result of responding to energy that intrudes into your personal space. You may turn to an electronic screen because of a signal you allow without considering how it may affect you. You may automatically pour yourself a glass of wine as soon as you get home, whether or not you really want it.

Sometimes the free flow of your energy is interrupted when you encounter a trigger, something activates frozen energy left over from a difficult situation from your past. Perhaps you overhear an annoyed parent speaking harshly to a child and you feel uncomfortable.

You may react by doing something to avoid your discomfort like getting angry at your companion for some small transgression or smoking a cigarette. If you learn to notice this reaction and use your discomfort as signal, though, you might remember what triggered this reaction: the sound of your father yelling at you. Then you can use the Logosynthesis sentences to release the energy frozen in that experience and reclaim it for your use now.

Noticing the experiences where your flowing energy is not guiding your actions is an important step toward noticing what really does allow you to enjoy the experience of having enough of what you want when you want it.

Enough Chocolate
Laurie: I have been playing with this idea for many years. I still practice this daily—with chocolate. My goal here is

to enjoy chocolate when I really want it instead of eating it automatically whenever I encounter it.

When I started this practice, I usually ate any chocolate offered to me immediately—and I struggled with a tendency to gain unwanted weight. Now, I keep a drawer in my kitchen filled with an assortment of my favorite types of chocolates. I find that I eat a small square or two almost every day. I savor it and feel content.

If I'm offered a variety of chocolate that is not among my favorites, I usually say, "no thanks" without any regret. I carry some of my favorites when I travel. I know I will always have more than enough.

The only time I have trouble maintaining my desired weight is when, for some reason, I stop attending to my own inner signals about food. When this happens, a frozen energy pattern is activated: I see the chocolate or other comfort food, grab it and eat it automatically. Once

I recognize this pattern, I can start paying attention to my healthy signals again.

Enough Pleasure

Willem: On a recent trip to Copenhagen, I noticed a repetitive pattern that won't surprise you. My wife and I like art and design, so we tend to visit museums and beautiful shops. Because I've been focusing on abundance for a while now, I noticed something interesting: Every time we entered a shop and I saw something beautiful, I immediately looked at the price, before even exploring the object.

That was a useful habit in the past because it helped me to avoid frustration: It didn't make sense to look at things I couldn't afford.

I started to practice looking at things without checking the price ticket first. That gave me an opportunity to look closer and to decide if this was really something I wanted to take with me. It usually wasn't, but the price didn't decide from the beginning anymore. Finally, I found a beautiful, horribly expensive shirt—for half the price.

Too Much Isn't Abundance Either

In order to experience abundance, you need to be able to experience enough.

When a group of workshop participants were asked what they experienced as scarce in their lives, answers included money, savings for retirement, time, space, help, education, appreciation, etc. In trying to define what *enough* would be, a new question arose—enough for what?

In the same workshop, answers to the question "What do you have too much of in your life?" focused on stuff. Paper, email, clutter, and collections of all kinds of things, were reported as detracting, not adding to anyone's experience of joy and satisfaction.

Accumulating too much is one way of trying to compensate for an experience of or a belief in scarcity.

> *I am realizing more & more that my happiness is tied to my money, so I try to soothe unhappiness with things. I am realizing that spending is bringing me no joy, in fact it's making me more aware of unhappiness in my life. I don't feel like I have enough even though I make a solid mid-range salary. I just feel really disconnected. And that can lead to further destruction. I am hoping this search will lead me to abundance.* PL

Accumulating too much may also be something you learn from someone else who experienced scarcity. You save things just in case you might need them some day.

Michel had trouble throwing things away. Magazines and reports were stacked in piles waiting to be read—when he had time. He realized how he had learned to save things when he helped his parents, who had lived through the great depression, when they moved to a smaller home.

He discovered that they had carefully saved every rubber band and paper clip. They had accumulated enough to last a small office for many years and enough band aids to stock a clinic. Bed linens and towels they didn't ever use were stuffed into the linen closet.

Wine and Other Stuff

Willem: I recently discovered a pattern that must be derived from an old experience of scarcity. I've learned to appreciate good wines, even though wine was not part of my upbringing. I have a wine cellar, and even though I've collected enough bottles for the next few years, I always feel uncomfortable if I see only a few empty racks in my stock. That's the moment I start looking around for opportunities to fill the gaps.

Laurie: I learned to save things from my own parents. Too much is uncomfortable—it makes it hard to find things when I want them. Shopping—buying more stuff at bargain prices—was a highly regarded skill in my family.

When I realized what I was doing, I devised the "How Much Is Enough" exercise that I used daily for many months to help me relearn how much is enough for me.

Practicing Abundance

Here are two different activities to help you find what is just right for you.

How Much is Enough?

Possible areas for exploration are listed below in no particular order:

> food, money, clothes, travel, contact with friends, study, writing, impact on others, email, fitness, exercise, hiking, grand mothering, clearing space, contemplation, giving/sharing, client contact, control, newspaper reading, shopping, email, novels, magazines, cooking, working, vacations, sex, alcohol, excitement, calmness, coffee, jewelry, sports equipment, screen time, cars, house, Xmas gifts, telephone time love,, movies, drugs,

medication, professional/activity, feelings, guilt, anger, suffering, agonizing, activities with children, eating out, watching TV, etc.

Fill in the blank with your choice of one of those topics. What is just enough_____for me?

Getting just enough for you leads to relaxation, satisfaction and happiness. Use this form to help you to think about what is just right for you.

Choose today's topic from our list, or create your own topic and start exploring the question: What is enough (space, money, eating out…etc.) for me right now?

How Much Is Enough?
Today's Topic: Enough _____
Today's Date _____

1. Why is it useful or important for me to think about this topic now?

2. How do I know when I have too much of this?
3. How do I know when I don't have enough of this?
4. What does my culture define as too much or not enough of this?
5. What did my family *say* about too much or not enough of this when I was a child? Now?
6. What did my family *do* about too much or not enough of this when I was a child? Now?
7. What was it like when I had just enough of this? Describe it. Or, if you have never experienced just enough of this, what do you imagine it would be like?
8. What does (or would) just enough of this look/feel like for me, now?
9. What action, if any, will I take to create just enough of this in my life? When?

You can use this exercise as often as you like for as long as you find it useful. We suggest that you use it daily for at least a week. Then decide whether to continue.

Chose Abundance Once

Your next challenge can be made into a delightful excursion. It is less structured but can still be an important way to learn what abundance means to you. It does involve spending money, but it can be done in a grocery store or anywhere else you like to shop.

Set aside more time than you think you will need for this one. Don't use it to do routine shopping. You will be going to a store for only one purpose. You are to choose and purchase something that you can easily afford that feels to you like it is a real luxury.

Shannon did this exercise and purchased one beautiful, out of season, pear and a box of expensive exotic tea bags, brought them home and thoroughly enjoyed the abundance she experienced.

Evan purchased a beautiful leather jacket that he wore frequently and enjoyed thoroughly. Your experience is up to you.

Chapter 7

Challenges: Beyond Not Enough and Too Much

Your financial life is influenced by a story you probably don't even know much about.

It's the story of what your life was going to be like that you created before you were 10 years old. You might have revised the story as a teenager and then forgotten about it, but there are various techniques available to help you rediscover it.

You created your story from many factors that included:

- what your caretakers said and did in your presence
- your understanding of and your reaction to that information
- the social circumstances that surrounded you
- your own age, temperament and resources
- decisions you made about how to respond to all these factors

These decisions may also relate to the times your life energy froze to protect yourself from situations you could not manage with your available resources.

Consequences of Triggering Frozen Life Energy

So long as you follow the script you created for your life story, you are probably fairly comfortable with it. But if you veer off your chosen path, you may encounter unexpected challenges.

Helena was very comfortable with her decision to enter medical school. Both of her parents were medical doctors and she had grown up just assuming that she would also become a doctor. Everything went smoothly and she spent about 20 years fulfilling what she believed was her destiny.

But when she felt forced to work under increasingly difficult circumstances as a doctor, she grew disillusioned with how her field had changed and seriously considered new opportunities outside of the medical profession. She struggled with her new impulses and became extremely uncomfortable and indecisive. She was trying to move outside her life story and meeting both internal and external resistance.

The external resistance came from family and colleagues urging her to keep practicing medicine. After all, she was so good at it, was well respected, had a secure income and so forth.

The internal resistance was more of a surprise. She imagined terrible scenarios of being destitute and losing the respect of and being shunned by her family and friends. She kept wanting to change but did nothing about it.

Helena, like most people, was unaware that she had frozen parts of herself that did not fit with her own and other people's expectations of her. It was these frozen parts that she had put aside to follow a narrow life path that others had rewarded her for choosing.

Now, new circumstances were triggering awareness of those frozen parts. The triggers, represented as frightening scenarios of the future, were now intruding into her wish to change her life.

Another way of describing this situation is that Helena had been doing what was expected of her throughout her life and was only now feeling the urge to listen to her true Self and discover her own mission or calling in the world.

Old Habits Create Scarcity

Lots of things in your life keep you from discovering your most important priorities. These are mostly outside expectations and the very real need to find enough money to meet your basic needs for food and shelter and other things you think will contribute to your comfort and well-being.

However, as philosopher Eric Hoffer said, "You can never get enough of what you don't need to make you happy."

The problem is that you have probably been surrounded by media messages giving you the opposite story. The message is, "You need this thing (whatever it may be) in order to be happy. Buy it now!"

This bombardment helps you create a fantasy that you should have more. This fantasy becomes even stronger if your family, work associates and friends all believe it, too, and compete to show off their latest acquisitions.

And if your financial prospects are limited because of circumstances beyond your control, you may feel even more deprived. You may create fantasies about what you should have and, perhaps, who is to blame because you don't have it.

If you can, you get so busy trying to earn enough money to buy the things you are brainwashed to believe you need that you feel anxious and stressed. You rarely stop to notice that the happiness you do find lasts for only a short time—because you can't ever experience enough of something when it isn't what you really need.

Trying to live this way, whether or not you are successful at getting enough money to acquire "stuff," creates a sense of scarcity. But if, like Helena, you've spent years in this pattern, changing can feel very threatening.

You Try to Fill the Void

If you have not sorted out your priorities and don't know what your life mission is, it is easy to get sidetracked and allow this outside energy to define you and what you believe you should have.

You try to solve the problem in ways that don't work and often make the problem worse. You keep trying to get enough of something to make you happy, but it does not help, because is not what you really need. (Knowing your life mission guides you to choose what you need to fulfil it.)

Collections

One common way to try to fill the void is to collect tangible things. Some people collect tools they never use. Others collect books they intend to read, but don't. Some collect kitchen gadgets, and some collect shoes.

> **Laurie**: Among the many things that I have collected over the years are coin proof sets.

Every year when the new coins became available, I would automatically order three new sets—one for me and one for each of my children. I would then put them into a drawer and forget about them until it was time to order the next sets.

Listening to a recording that challenged the purpose of collections finally brought me to my senses.

What are you collecting and buying automatically that you don't use or enjoy? It may be useful to notice what outside energy influenced you to start your collection and whether using the Logosynthesis sentences would help you let them go.

You may try to fill the void with activity like entertainment that does nothing but distract you. You may mindlessly watch whatever electronic screen is available and then be too busy or tired to learn the information or do the real work of creating the financial stability or wealth you dream about.

You may even choose to numb yourself with alcohol or drugs, hoping you won't notice the pain of this void.

And all the while, you are carrying out the script for the life story you created when you were a child about how your life was going to develop.

The Way Out

As you try to learn to navigate the world it is natural to lose your connection to your Self. However, if you are lucky enough to notice this void, you can start your search to reclaim these connections as an adult. You probably don't know that this is what you are doing. You just know that, somehow, you aren't satisfied and are searching for something else.

That something, at its core, is your true Self, your connection to Essence and your own mission, the work you were meant to do in this world.

The more closely you approach these objectives, the more likely you will be to experience the abundance you are searching for. Following the suggestions in this book is part of your journey.

It is much easier to set priorities when you use this guideline. Will choosing this over something else move me closer to my mission in the world?

Here There Be Dragons...

Of course, this is likely to also bring up the kind of resistance that Helena encountered. Each time you do something that makes you less likely to follow someone else's energy rather than your own, the frozen parts of you that were trying to protect you are triggered. You may experience memories and fantasies that make your new path seem extra dangerous or less rewarding.

That is where the tools you have been learning will be most helpful. Each time you encounter the resistance, using the Logosynthesis sentences will help you move through it to release your frozen energy to create greater bandwidth and energy to accomplish your new goals.

Using Logosynthesis Tools to Reclaim Your Frozen Energy

Here are two stories of work done by participants in one of Willem's workshops. Both stories include using the Logosynthesis sentences.

Sarah

Sarah kept finding reasons to avoid taking more responsibility in her company. She was puzzled about her reluctance because she definitely had the skills needed to manage those new challenges.

Finally, she realized that she was reacting to an old message from her father who mistrusted people with money. Her new job responsibilities would bring her more income. Her father had led her to believe, "If you have money, you are bad."

She said the three Logosynthesis sentences using "the value system of my father" as the trigger phase. She felt immediate relief, smiled and decided to move forward in her career.

Sarah's sentences:
1. *I retrieve all my energy bound up in (the value system of my father) and take it to the right place in my Self.*
2. *I remove all non-me energy related to (the value system of my father) from all of my cells, my body and my personal space and send it to where it truly belongs.*
3. *I retrieve my energy bound up in all my reactions to (the value system of my father) and take it to the right place in my Self.*

Felix

Felix was reluctant to move from the dental clinic where he worked into the private practice he dreamed about. He kept imagining himself as not having enough money to survive. Then he remembered concluding, "I am not enough" when he was only 3 years old and his mother looked at him in a particular way.

When he said the sentences about his trigger, "my mother's eyes and all they represent," he felt very relaxed. The image of his mother disappeared and then the fantasy of being homeless and being seen and shamed by others emerged.

When he used the trigger of "the faces of these people who are shaming me," in the Logosynthesis sentences, his fear almost disappeared. He was ready to continue toward on to creating his own dream and opening his own private dental practice.

Felix's first set of sentences using 'my mother's eyes and all they represent' as the triggering phrase.

1. *I retrieve all my energy bound up in (my mother's eyes and all they represent) and take it to the right place in my Self.*
2. *I remove all non-me energy related to (my mother's eyes and all they represent) from all of my cells, my body and my personal space and send it to where it truly belongs.*
3. *I retrieve my energy bound up in all my reactions to (my mother's eyes and all they represent) and take it to the right place in my Self.*

Felix's second set of sentences using 'the faces of these people who are shaming me' as the triggering phrase.

1. *I retrieve all my energy bound up in (the faces of these people who are shaming) me and take it to the right place in my Self.*
2. *I remove all non-me energy related to (the faces of these people who are shaming) me from all of my cells, my body and my personal space and send it to where it truly belongs.*

3. I retrieve my energy bound up in all my reactions to (the faces of these people who are shaming me) and take it to the right place in my Self.

Practicing Abundance

What do you do now instead of taking action to fulfil your own mission? It could be anything from collecting things, to spending money instead of saving or investing it, abusing alcohol or drugs or playing games on the internet or something else entirely.

You do not need to share this information with anyone else—it is just for your own awareness.

What do you see, hear, feel or imagine that triggers this avoiding behavior?

Condense that trigger into a few words as you learned to do in Chapter 5. Then insert those words into the Logosynthesis sentences using Sarah's and Felix's sentences as a model.

Say the sentences aloud—or with the help of a friend. Take your time and notice what happens when you do this.

1. *I retrieve all my energy bound up in (your trigger phrase) and take it to the right place in my Self.*
2. *I remove all non-me energy related to (your trigger phrase) from all of my cells, my body and my personal space and send it to where it truly belongs.*
3. *I retrieve my energy bound up in all my reactions to (your trigger phrase) and take it to the right place in my Self.*

If a second trigger emerges, repeat the process. If you feel that the problem has been resolved, say the final sentence, "*I tune all of my systems to this new awareness.*"

Note: The most challenging part of learning to use Logosynthesis is often finding your trigger phrases. It is not a precise process. Remember, if you would like more samples of triggers used to resolve issues around scarcity, money and related issues, you can download them here: **www.BooksbyLaurie.com/triggers**.

You can also see 50 samples of trigger phrases in Chapter 6 of *Letting It Go*. Meanwhile, just relax and practice—the worst thing that can happen is nothing. If that happens, just experiment with using a different phrase.

Chapter 8

The Mystery of Money

Do you remember how you learned about money? Were you given coins as a child? Was money a toy or a tool? Did you hear grownups talking about it with worried voices? Were you instructed in "the value of money?"

Deliberate Confusion

Laurie: As a 10-year-old, I remember watching the grownups at an extended family gathering confuse my 2-year-old brother about money with a coin exchange game. They used US coins: a copper penny is larger than a silver colored dime that is worth 10 pennies. A silver colored nickel, worth 5 pennies, is larger than a penny.

The grownups knew the relative values of the coins. The 2-year-old was much more interested in the size, color and quantity of the coins. He was quite happy to be the center of attention and play the exchange game with them.

Someone offered him a dime, which he happily accepted. Then someone else offered to exchange the dime for a larger, but less valuable nickel. He liked the bigger coin and took it, and everyone laughed at a joke he did not understand.

Then someone else offered to exchange two coins, pennies, that had still less value for the nickel. Again, he happily accepted the new coins and the grownups laughed uproariously. This time he seemed confused by the laughter.

I am not sure if this event had any particular impact on him, but I know he struggled with managing money throughout most of his life.

Clear Guidelines

Willem: The amount of pocket money for the children in my family depended on age: If you were older, you got more. I remember being very proud when I became ten years old, because I finally got 25 cents of a Dutch guilder every week.

Strangely enough this pattern has been repeated by society. Until I retired, I earned more money every year in my jobs and in my business.

My parents were very clear that I had to save money. I was allowed to freely spend half of what I got, and I had to save the other half for bigger wishes. Gifts came only on birthdays and from Santa Claus, but if we wanted something during the year, we had to save for it from our pocket money.

Later I learned that I could earn money by doing something for it, like delivering newspapers or working in a factory during the summer holidays. I've continued this pattern. I've always saved a pretty big part of my income, and I have never had to borrow any money, apart from a mortgage for a house.

Mixed Messages
Laurie: My personal experience was much like Willem's. I, too, had to save, especially once I started to earn money as a teenager, and that money was earmarked for my education. I learned early to use credit wisely and pay off my credit card debts each month.

My husband learned different lessons. He was permitted to spend whatever he earned. Our children struggled to integrate the different money messages they received, as they grew into adulthood.

It is no wonder that we have so many different answers to the question "Just what is money anyhow, and what am I supposed to do with it?"

Money is completely neutral by itself, but it has different meanings to different people in different situations. Even historians disagree about the origin, uses and meanings of money in human history.

Money is a Thing

One helpful story, which archeologists say is untrue, says simply, "money is coconuts." It talks about the development of coins, paper money and banks.

The story is that people on an island liked coconuts and, once-upon-a-time, bartered with each other for goods and services. Something like this: you, Tom, help me build my hut and I, Dick, will help you clear your field.

Then, things got more complicated. Dick was happy to help Tom but didn't need help with his field; instead, Tom needed new sandals. Harry needed help clearing his field and was also a good sandal maker. To solve the problem, Dick offered Tom a coconut in exchange for help with the hut. Then Tom gave the coconut to Harry in exchange for new sandals. Harry, in turn, gave Dick the coconut and Dick helped Harry clear the field.

However, on this island, some people liked to work more than others and accumulated large sacks of coconuts that were hard to haul around. Then Sylvia offered a solution to that problem. She offered to store the coconuts in a large cave and give a small piece of metal in exchange to prove that she had a coconut in storage. Eventually, people used the small metal as payments instead of the coconuts that were stored in Sylvia's cave.

Money Represents Energy

While this story isn't based on actual events, it does represent something else that is quite useful. Money is a symbol: it refers to life energy in different forms than you may usually recognize.

It is a symbol for the energy expended to build the hut, clear the field and make the sandals. It is also a symbol for the life energy expended to entertain people, to teach important information, to grow food, to solve problems and for a myriad of other things.

Money then can be understood as a storage place for life energy. The life energy in this money can be free, like cash or a savings account you can access at any time, perhaps from a bank cash machine. We can spend that money immediately for whatever we want to use it for.

Life energy can also be bound in money used to purchase a house or a car. That money is stored energy dedicated to a certain purpose and isn't easily available to be transformed into something else.

Currently unavailable money holds stored energy that has the potential to be released later. It exists because of an agreement. It's not accessible right now but will be later, like a payment that is owed to you for completed work. The promise of future retirement benefits also fits this category.

Of course, depending upon who is defining it, money is much more than these things.

How Authorities Define Money

Money is a current medium of exchange in the form of coins and banknotes. Money is coins and banknotes collectively. *Webster Dictionary*

Money is any item or verifiable record that is generally accepted as payment for goods and services and repayment of debts, such as taxes, in a particular country or socio-economic context. *Wikipedia*

Money is any good that is widely used and accepted in transactions involving the transfer of goods and services from one person to another. *CliffsNotes*

That seems to include coconuts, coins, shells, gold nuggets, ball point pens (in India in 1986 a ball point pen was worth 3 bananas), paper currency, and paper as well as electronic records such as bitcoins.

How Ordinary People Define Money

Laurie: As I was drafting this chapter, I decided to do some informal research about this question. So, of course I opened Facebook and asked for a quick answer to the question, "What is money?" There were 83 responses.

I also started asking people I encountered and tabulating their answers as well. I collected about 100 responses to this question. Here is a summary. The numbers add up to more than 100 because some individual's responses fell into more than one category.

30 people referred to money as a way of exchanging one thing for another. 18 saw it as a form of energy. Another 8 saw it as a tool and 6 more as a symbol or representation of something else. Only 7 called it a concrete thing: cash or currency.

Others seemed to focus on what money represented in their lives. These were change (or the ability to effect change) 8, security 6, freedom 5, survival 4, quality of life 2. A single person said money is abundance and one other responded that money is love!

Another 16 responded with a judgement of some kind. Some were clearly negative: money is dirty, shit, the root of all evil and inequalities, a weapon of the powerful, a nuisance, a distraction, a source of divisions, and a source of worry, jealousy, fraud and manipulation.

Other judgements were more ambivalent: A blessing and a curse, an overvalued but necessary resource in this world, mirrored perceptions, and something momentarily owned but not eternally yours.

The Origin of Money

The truth is, nobody really knows. In the book, *Debt - Updated and Expanded: The First 5,000 Years* by David Graeber, the author provides evidence that money was originally invented to measure a debt one owed the King.

He also suggests that primitive societies did not barter for goods and services but used some form of currency (cattle, metal, shells) as a way of measuring the worth of a human life. This could be the price of a bride or what one owed as compensation to the family of someone who was killed.

Money is a Relative Measurement

Being a millionaire was once thought to be a measure of great wealth in the US. Now the suggested amount of savings to have for a comfortable middle-class retirement in the US is 2.4 million dollars. (Fewer than 10% of families achieve this milestone.)

Laurie: My husband and I have lived in our home for nearly 50 years. We paid a certain amount for the house. Now our community's assessment of the value of this house (in money) is 17 times what we originally paid for it. It is the same building, albeit with some necessary repairs and upgrades.

A new car now costs about as much as the original amount we paid for the house. And clients pay me 7-12 times what I used to charge for an hour-long session.

Adapting to these changes is sometimes a challenge for me and I remind myself that this money I am spending reflects changing numbers on a piece of paper. My life is abundant, regardless of what measurement I use.

Useful Ideas About Money that Encourage Experiencing Abundance

Money is a NEUTRAL way of measuring and comparing value.

Money is stored life energy. Energy can be neither created nor destroyed. It can only be changed from one form to another. This is the first law of thermodynamics—a physical constant in the universe.

Money is a replaceable commodity. This is true so long as you have life energy available to transform into something that is useful to others.

You can store life energy for later use in the form of money.

Money management is a skill that you can learn. In the next chapter we'll describe many strategies for learning this skill.

Practicing Abundance

Take a realistic measure of the amount of money you have available to you right now. This is a snapshot, not a movie.

If you are reacting to this suggestion with anxiety or anger or are thinking of reasons you can't possibly do this now, use the 3 Logosynthesis sentences to retrieve your energy for this task. Use "the idea of measuring my money" as the trigger.

Now, back to the task. This is just about measuring money, not measuring the value of all your possessions—that is called measuring your net worth and this task is just a part of that measurement.

This means listing the amount of money you have in your pocket or purse and the amount of money you have in your bank account(s). Include everything, such as an uncashed check or Paypal balance, that can be easily converted to cash. Add these numbers.

Now make a list of money you have already spent but not yet deducted from these bank balances. That includes money owed to others for goods and services you have already received. These numbers are found in bills and receipts that may be scattered around your physical and virtual space. Add these numbers as well.

Subtract what you owe from what you have and notice if the number is positive (you have more money than you owe others) or negative (you need additional money to pay your debts.)

If you experience stress at any point during this process, identify the triggers of that stress and use the Logosynthesis sentences to regain your equilibrium.

Acknowledging the truth about your financial situation is one of the most important steps in creating the abundance provided by financial stability in your life.

Chapter 9

The Mastery of Money— An Introduction

Releasing your energy from old, limiting beliefs and experiences about money does not mean you will automatically have a successful financial life. These beliefs and experiences have probably interfered with your interest in and ability to acquire the information you need to reach your financial goals.

If you already have information about managing your finances and creating wealth, but blocked energy has kept you from using it, go ahead and use what you already know—and stay open to acquiring new information. If you have missed this information in the past, for whatever reason, it's now time to learn about managing your financial life.

Neither of us are financial professionals, so please consider this chapter a beginning. Rather than offering you financial advice, we will suggest avenues of learning we have traveled and share some of our experiences along the way.

Nearly boundless resources for acquiring information surround you. Choosing which will be most useful to you may seem overwhelming. We'll point you to those that have been most helpful to us. However, our advice is no substitute for finding competent professional advisors when you are ready for them. We will offer you some guidelines about doing that as well.

Recognizing Potential Problems

It's easy to fall into money traps and much harder to get out of them.

Jeremy fell into the student loan trap. His parents were not able to help him pay his college expenses and he knew that he could not earn enough to manage them himself. The school he attended offered a loan program and he took full advantage of it. He graduated thousands of dollars in debt.

His low paying, entry level job provided barely enough money to live comfortably, and he made only minimal payments on those loans for several years. He despaired of ever paying off the debts or accumulating enough money to buy a house or support a family.

Teri was offered a credit card immediately after enrolling in college. Thrilled, she accepted without considering her ability to pay her monthly bill. She regularly used the credit card to pay for activities she could not otherwise afford. When she graduated, she also felt overwhelmed by the burden of this debt. However, by living extremely frugally for several years, she managed to pay it off and regain her freedom.

Miranda and **Peter** accepted an invitation from a friend to learn about an amazing investment opportunity. The presenter painted a rosy picture of the expected outcome of this investment and cautioned that the window of opportunity to make this investment would soon close.

Their friend announced his intention to invest and encouraged them to take advantage of this opportunity while it was still available. They had no time to talk over their decision with anyone else and decided to invest a modest amount. After 2 years of inquiries about the progress of the project they learned that the investment had been a scam all along and that they could not recover any of their money.

These are just a few stories of the types of uninformed decisions that can lead you into falsely concluding that you just can't win when it comes to mastering the money game. You may have your own stories and have come to similar conclusions.

If you have, reclaim your energy from these situations by using the Logosynthesis sentences and get ready for a fresh start.

Wealth and Abundance

Mastering money can be understood as a game with its own definitions and rules. One goal of this game is to produce wealth. Wealth is money and the things it can buy, that you keep and use throughout your life. When you use this wealth in a way that is congruent with your life's purpose you experience abundance.

Accumulating wealth can also lead to financial independence. When you are financially independent the wealth you have accumulated produces enough money to cover your regular living expenses and you no longer need to earn additional money by working.

How anyone does this may seem like a mystery to you now. Certainly, neither of us understood it at the beginnings of our journeys. One series of allegories that explain the journey clearly is found in the 1926 book, *The Richest Man in Babylon* by George S. Clason.

In this story, set in ancient Babylon, a rich man mentors a young man and slowly teaches him the rules to creating wealth. These rules are just as valid today as they were nearly 100 years ago, which probably accounts for the continuing popularity of the book and the many summaries of it available online.

Your chances of successfully producing wealth depend upon you understanding and following the time-honored guidelines included in Clason's book and most other books on financial success. We list several other books we like later in this chapter.

Critical Fundamental Information

Basically, there are only a limited number of things you can do with money.

- You can earn money.
- You can spend money.
- You can save money.
- You can invest money.

There are an infinite variety of ways to do each of those things, but these are the basics.

You could choose to borrow money in order to spend or invest it. Sometimes this can be useful and sometimes it will lead to unexpected problems. It's best to listen to sound professional advice before you do this.

In any case, borrowed money cannot count as wealth. You must repay it with money you earn or acquire in some other way, perhaps as a gift. However, that gift is available only because someone else has earned, saved or invested money.

Laurie's Experiment

When I first started to learn about money, I encountered this revolutionary affirmation, "Part of all I earn is mine to keep." Until that day (sometime in 1976), it had never occurred to me that anything other than earning money, saving it to spend later or spending it immediately were possible. I had never considered the possibility of deliberately achieving financial independence. In fact, I don't think I even knew what those words meant.

This adult education class also came with a set of instructions about how to start my own journey toward financial independence. It was designed to deliberately focus my awareness on making conscious decisions about money and ultimately having enough money to live comfortably without working.

I chose to follow these simple instructions.

Each time you receive money put it into 4 different savings accounts—each with its own set of guidelines. (This was before the days of outrageously high bank fees. Using this method today probably would cost much less if you use just one account and keep careful records of each pot of money.)

1. **Income**: Deposit all the money you receive into this account and transfer it from there into all your other accounts. This includes a checking account you use for everyday purchases and the other savings accounts. The rule for this account was "*always take out less than you put in.*"
2. **Financial Independence**: Deposit a regular percentage of your income into this interest-bearing

account. The rules for this account were "*never take out the deposited money but always take out the interest and spend it consciously for your own benefit.*" The goal of this account was to eventually have enough interest to live on.

3. **Large Purchase**: Deposit extra money into this account. The rule for this account is to "*spend it all on purchases that bring you personal pleasure.*"
4. **Investment**: Deposit whatever you choose into this account. This rule is "*only take money out when it will be reinvested at a higher yield.*"

What Happened Still Amazes Me

In the first year I managed to add $1000 to my Financial Independence account and spent the small amount of interest on an ice cream treat. Then, sometime in 1977, I read a book that jolted me into awareness of investing. It was the first book I had ever found that clearly explained the basic mechanics of investing. I was so excited that I read it twice within 3 days of receiving it!

Reading *The Joy of Money: The Guide to Women's Financial Freedom* by Paula Nelson changed my life. I very carefully selected a top-rated mutual fund, opened my first investment account and started keeping records.

I made my first $1000 investment in 1978, my second in 1979 and my third a year later in 1980—a total of $3000. I arranged to have all dividends (the equivalent of interest) sent to me. Ten years later I had received checks totaling $6850 and my original investment was worth more than $3000.

I have not made any changes to that original investment account and have continued to receive checks twice a year. The checks vary in amount because of variations in the stock market, as does the dollar value of the original account. Each check, money that comes to me to be spent purely for my own pleasure, provides a new experience of abundance.

Since my first investment, I have collected a total of $23,000 in cash and the value of the account is currently about $10,000 (which is about equivalent to $3000 in 1977 dollars).

While I was carefully accumulating small amounts of money for this experiment, a professional friend suggested that my husband and I enroll in a new workshop, Money and You: Management by Agreement. What we learned there both affirmed and challenged our old views of creating wealth. It led us on a 5-year adventure of experimenting with new ideas and sharing our excitement with others.

After some misadventures and hard lessons about focusing on wealth building activities instead of our work as psychotherapists, we decided to focus our energy on doing the moderately paying work we love.

We turned over the difficult investment and money management work we did not fully understand to a skilled financial adviser. Following his advice allows us to enjoy our financial independence now.

Willem Followed a Different Path

Willem: When my wife Luzia and I were recently reading an article online by Tom Corley, entitled "*16 Rich Habits*," we realized that we had done a lot of what he described as a way to achieve wealth. I'm quoting our seven most important habits from Tom Corley's list. They're boringly unspectacular, but they've worked.

- Live within your means.
- Don't gamble.
- Read every day.
- Network and volunteer regularly.
- Don't give up.
- Get a mentor.
- Eliminate "bad luck" from your vocabulary.
- Know your main purpose.

This is a Lifelong Journey
Reading this book is a start. If you have done the "Practicing Abundance" activities, continue with these suggestions. If you have not yet done those activities, start now.

The process may seem overwhelming. Take it at a pace that works for you. Remember the often-retold story of eating an elephant one bite at a time.

Delay working on your finances until you reclaim the energy that comes from releasing your old blocking beliefs. That will help you create enough bandwidth to manage these tasks.

If any of these suggestions triggers a negative reaction for you, use the Logosynthesis sentences to reclaim your energy from that trigger before you try to go further.

Start Where You Are
Taking the time to understand your current financial status in an excellent place to start the next phase of your

journey. You calculated your available cash in your last activity. Calculating your monetary net worth, the value of everything you own minus the value of everything you owe, is another useful exercise.

You may need courage to do this and discover the extent of your debts. The Logosynthesis process you have learned will help you manage this very, very important step. Just type 'calculate personal net worth' into any search engine online and follow the instructions to get started.

Once you complete this process you will know whether you are currently in a positive financial position or whether you need to pay off debts to achieve this position. Again, there are many resources available to teach you how to do this—one step at a time.

Remember to use the Logosynthesis process whenever you have difficulty with anything you encounter. This journey takes time for everyone. You don't need to become an expert overnight.

Books Laurie Recommends
How to Get Out of Debt, Stay Out of Debt, and Live Prosperously*: Based on the Proven Principles and Techniques of Debtors Anonymous, is a classic favorite book by Jerrold Mundis that is extremely useful. So is *Your Money or Your Life: 9 Steps to Transforming Your Relationship with Money and Achieving Financial Independence: Fully Revised and Updated for 2018* by Vicki Robin, Joe Dominguez, et al.

If you need help increasing your income try following the suggestions in *Moneylove: How to Get the Money You Deserve for Whatever You Want* by Jerry Gillies. Another useful book is *Money Is My Friend* by Phil Laut, et al.

Have Fun Along the Way!
Children learn by playing and you can, too. Robert T. Kiyosaki, author of *Rich Dad Poor Dad: What the Rich Teach Their Kids About Money That the Poor and Middle Class Do Not!,* and his team invented a brilliant board

game, CASHFLOW®. Play it to learn many aspects of financial literacy, investing and becoming financially independent. Again—use a search engine to learn where you can purchase it.

Playing regularly with a group of like-minded friends can teach you more than you can imagine. But be warned, playing this game can take several hours and once you start, you probably won't want to stop until you have completed the game. One young man invited his friends for an early afternoon game, but they ended up staying past 11pm.

If you would prefer an intensive, mind-expanding experience, The Money and You® workshop is still available, too.

Get Help When You Need It

It is normal to use professional help to navigate the complexities of the world. You probably have used the services of a doctor, a lawyer, a plumber, an account, a pilot and a host of other specialists to do things you are not skilled enough to do yourself. Sooner than you think, you'll also need a professional or group of professionals to help you manage your financial affairs.

As when choosing any professional to work with, be sure the one you pick is both ethical and competent. They should be happy to show you their credentials and explain the meaning of all those letters. You definitely need to choose someone who subscribes to an ethical system that puts your needs ahead of their desire to sell you something.

You can and should ask others who are financially successful for their recommendations, but don't just accept someone else's judgement. Enter 'choosing a financial advisor' into a search engine and read an article that will give you information about types of advisors and the meaning of their credentials. This is an important decision, so take your time and make it carefully.

Your Next Steps

The difference between learning about abundance and experiencing abundance is like the difference between seeing a picture of an ice cream cone and actually eating an ice cream cone.

You may experience trouble at the border. You may find that you intend to do something but have trouble getting started. You aren't alone. Now you have new tools that will help you to get to the other side of this energy barrier. Remember to use them!

Carry a copy of the Logosynthesis sentences with you. You can download a copy to photograph and keep on your phone at **www.BooksByLaurie.com/guide**.

The Logosynthesis process you have learned has helped each of us make that transition many times. Use it each time you feel blocked and enjoy the experience of abundance in all areas of your life.

What we have written about Logosynthesis in this book is only a part of the story. Logosynthesis is also a great instrument to clarify your goals in life and to overcome negative emotions, disturbing memories and limiting beliefs. If you want to know more, find our other books online, wherever books are sold.

We Need Your Help

If you have found reading *Embrace Prosperity: Resolve Blocks to Experiencing Abundance* valuable, will you help others learn about it?

Most people choose a book because someone they trust recommends it or because of reviews they encounter. We would really appreciate it if you became one of those people who helps others by sharing your experience.

It is as easy as telling friends about it. **Just tell them one or two things you found valuable about it and why.**

If you are more ambitious, you can share what your biggest concern or problem was before reading this book and what you learned that helped you address it differently. You can even share what you wish had been different about the book.

Post a review—Please! It is almost as easy as talking to a friend. Just write those few things in a few sentences and post them wherever you read your reviews. Amazon, Goodreads, your own blog, or wherever books are sold.

If writing is a challenge, you can dictate those sentences into the Notes app on your phone, copy the note and post that.

To make it easier for you, here's a link to Laurie's author page on Amazon, **www.BooksByLaurie.com**. Just click on any book cover image and it will take you to the page where you can leave a review.

> With gratitude and appreciation,
> Laurie & Willem
> Dr. Laurie Weiss & Dr. Willem Lammers

P.S. If you take an extra few minutes to let me know where and when you post your review, I will personally thank you for helping us reach new readers. Just drop me an email at LaurieWeiss@EmpowermentSystems.com.

LOGOSYNTHESIS RESOURCES

LIA - Logosynthesis International Association
www.logosynthesis.international is an independent, international non-profit organization based in Switzerland.

The LIA:

- supports professionals and other interested parties with Logosynthesis®
- establishes a worldwide Logosynthesis® network with numerous active hubs
- offers a platform for the exchange of knowledge and experience
- contributes to the spreading of Logosynthesis®
- promotes the quality and further development of Logosynthesis
- certifies professionals across various levels

LIA members are trained specialists from counselling, educational and medical professions.

Books

Letting It Go: Relieve Anxiety and Toxic Stress in Just a Few Minutes Using Only Words (Rapid Relief with Logosynthesis®) is an easy introduction to Logosynthesis.

Self Coaching with Logosynthesis® is more about self coaching.

Logosynthesis®: Healing with Words: A Handbook for the Helping Professions is in-depth information for professionals.

Minute Miracles. The Practice of Logosynthesis®. Inspiration from Real Life contains many examples from Willem's practice.

Additional Logosynthesis books are listed by LIA and this list is updated regularly as new books become available. www.logosynthesis.international/publications/

Social Media
Facebook Group:
www.Facebook.com/groups/logosynthesis/

This is an open public group for people interested in knowing about Logosynthesis® events worldwide, and for newcomers to ask questions.

Facebook Group Logosynthesis Trainees E:
www.facebook.com/groups/324282328113524/

This is an advanced group open by application for helping professionals who have completed at least the Basic Introductory course.

There are other Facebook groups in different languages, e.g. Logosynthèse, Logosintesi, and Logosynthese.

Training Opportunities
Current offerings are announced in the Facebook Logosynthesis group and listed at www.logosynthesis.net/online and www.logosynthesis.international/calendar/

Acknowledgements

It takes a village to create a book!

I am grateful for the help of many people for their support, encouragement and insight that has brought this book from an idea to a reality.

Many, many, many thanks to:

- Dr. Willem Lammers, whose development of Logosynthesis opened a whole new chapter for my professional development. I am honored that he invited me to bring my expertise in translating complicated concepts into accessible language to collaborating with him on this project.

- Dr. Jonathan B. Weiss, my husband since 1960 and business partner since 1972, for reading every word of the first draft of each chapter and helping with so many of the other technical and tedious tasks that are necessary to produce a book.

- My beta-readers, Kaja Katarina Baumann, Foster Brashear, Charles Clark, Alan RY, Sandra Rusch, Judy Sabah, Jeannette Seibly and Virna Trivellato, whose specific feedback was incredibly helpful in crafting the final form of this book.

- The members of the Logosynthesis Facebook group who have offered support and feedback from so many different perspectives and countries!

- The participants on the JimBoat 8 who helped clarify so many final details about offering this material to the entrepreneur community.

Willem adds his special thanks to Lara Cardona-Morisset for her support in the development of the online abundance program and to the participants in this program for their contributions.

Finally, thank you for the invaluable advice and support of Judith Briles and all my friends and colleagues at AuthorU.org throughout every phase of this project.

Laurie
Dr. Laurie Weiss

About the Authors
Dr. Laurie Weiss

After over 40 years practicing psychotherapy and coaching, Dr. Laurie Weiss had no intention of starting a new phase of her career. Then a colleague helped her resolve a persistent, stressful problem using an amazing new technique. She was astounded that he did it in just a few minutes, while standing on the sidewalk outside of a restaurant, using only words.

Dr. Weiss was so intrigued with this recently discovered tool that she and her husband of over fifty years, Dr. Jonathan B. Weiss, went to Nova Scotia, Canada to learn the technique. Using it, they were thrilled to help their clients make important life changes in a fraction of the time, and with a fraction of the pain ordinarily associated with psychotherapy.

Now, ten years later, she is a Certified Logosynthesis Trainer and Master Practitioner and the author of a popular introductory Logosynthesis book. She is delighted to have collaborated with Dr. Lammers, the developer of this powerful method, on this project.

Dr. Weiss has long believed that ordinary people can learn to help themselves solve all kinds of problems if only they have the right tools. Throughout her professional life as an expert in Business and Personal Relationship Communication, Developmentally Based Psychotherapy and Transactional Analysis, she has specialized in making those tools accessible to anyone who is interested.

She brings to this, her thirteenth book, her expertise in writing in a way that makes complex professional information usable by ordinary people.

She and her husband live and work in Littleton, Colorado, USA.

How to Work with Dr. Laurie Weiss

My husband, Dr. Jonathan B. Weiss, and I have been married since 1960 and have been business partners since 1972 when we were teaching Transactional Analysis throughout the United States. We have been learning and teaching cutting-edge tools for healing and transformation for over 40 years.

Currently we are the only Certified Master Logosynthesis Practitioners in the United States. Either or both of us would be delighted to help you learn more about Logosynthesis and how to use it in your life and work.

Contact Us: We Usually Answer the Phone

You can contact us directly to discuss what is best for you and your group. We offer a variety of options including CLASSES, TALKS, BOOK GROUP VISITS, PROFESSIONAL CONFERENCE PRESENTATIONS, TRAINING, and

INDIVIDUAL APPOINTMENTS. We work with our clients in person, by phone and online.

Dr. Laurie Weiss:
LaurieWeiss@EmpowermentSystems.com

Dr. Jonathan Weiss:
Weiss@EmpowermentSystems.com

Empowerment Systems
506 West Davies Way
Littleton, CO 80120 USA
303.794.5379

Websites
Personal—www.LaurieWeiss.com
Logosynthesis—www.LogosynthesisColorado.com
Business—www.EmpowermentSystems.com
Purchase Books— www.BooksbyLaurie.com

Social Media

Facebook—www.Facebook.com/laurieweiss

LinkedIn—www.Linkedin.com/in/laurieweiss

Pinterest— www.Pinterest.com/laurieweiss/

Twitter—Twitter.com/@LaurieWeiss

Goodreads—www.Goodreads.com/Laurie_Weiss

Instagram—www.Instagram.com/drlaurieweiss

Blogs

Personal Development—
www.IDontNeedTherapy.com/blog

Relationship—RelationshipHQ.com/blog/

Business Communication—
http://www.DareToSayIt.com

About the Authors
Dr. Willem Lammers

Dr. Willem Lammers is a Swiss psychologist, psychotherapist, coach and consultant to organizations with 40+ years of experience in the field.

Trained in Transactional Analysis, Gestalt therapy, hypnotherapy, NLP and different modalities of energy psychology, he has held positions at a university and in a hospital and founded his own institute. He has trained professionals in psychotherapy, coaching, supervision and organizational development.

While searching for a more elegant, effective and direct way to guide people through their pain and into their development, he became increasingly aware that we are more than our physical body and our mind. In 2005 he discovered Logosynthesis® and now trains professionals in this new, simple but effective model for self-coaching, counselling and psychotherapy.

In 2014, Willem co-founded the Logosynthesis International Association, which is now responsible for certifying professionals in Logosynthesis as both practitioners and trainers of this rapidly spreading, elegant model.

In 2018, Dr. Lammers received the prestigious ACEP Award for his major contribution to the field of energy psychology. He publishes books and articles in German, Italian, Dutch, Serbian and English. This is his eighth book.

He lives in Maienfeld GR, Switzerland and trains and consults with professionals around the world.

How to Work with Dr. Willem Lammers

Dr. Lammers offers online courses and occasional lectures and classes in various locations around the world. He also frequently participates in the Facebook Logosynthesis discussion group at Facebook.com/logosynthesis.

Visit The Origin of Logosynthesis® for a variety of resources: www.logosynthesis.net/

This is the website of Dr. Willem Lammers' personal training institute. Here you can find extensive resources with links to other resources at LIA as well as his current teaching schedule.

Dr. Willem Lammers: info@Logosynthesis.net

OTHER BOOKS BY DR. LAURIE WEISS

Letting It Go: Relieve Anxiety and Toxic Stress in Just a Few Minutes Using Only Words (Rapid Relief with Logosynthesis®)
Are you ready for relaxation to replace anxiety in your life?
(Also available in German)

Secrets of Happy Relationship Series

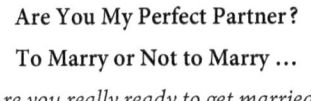

Are You My Perfect Partner?
To Marry or Not to Marry …
Are you really ready to get married?

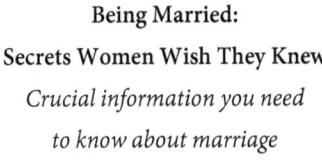

Being Married:
Secrets Women Wish They Knew
Crucial information you need to know about marriage

Relationship Tips for Life Partners
Critical guidelines for creating a true partnership

**Stop Poisoning Your Marriage
with These Common Beliefs**
*Are you letting these myths
undermine your marriage?*

**Reconnect to Rescue Your Marriage:
Avoid Divorce and Feel Loved Again**
What to do before leaving your troubled marriage

**Stop Arguing and Start Talking …
even if you are afraid your only
answer is divorce!**
*Are you ready to have these loving,
productive conversations with your spouse?*

OTHER BOOKS BY LAURIE WEISS

**Being Happy Together:
What to Do to Keep Love Alive**
*Unlock secrets to rapid relationship
renewal in just an hour a week*

Additional Books

**Emotional Self-Help: I Don't Need Therapy,
But Where Do I Turn for Answers?**
Do you need to become emotionally literate?

**Recovery From CoDependency:
It's Never Too Late To Reclaim Your Childhood**
Are you ready to release your codependency?

An Action Plan for Your Inner Child:
Parenting Each Other
Are you ready to reclaim your inner child?

What Is the Emperor Wearing?
Truth-Telling in Business Relationships
Do you wish you dared to tell the truth?
(Also available in German and Chinese)

OTHER BOOKS BY
DR. WILLEM LAMMERS

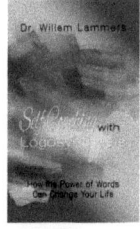

Self-Coaching with Logosynthesis

(Also available in German, Serbian and Italian)

Logosynthesis Handbook

for the Helping Professions

(Also available in German and Dutch)

Minute Miracles. The Practice ofLogosynthesis.

Inspiration from Real Life

(Also available in German)

You Don't Make Me Feel. States of Mind in Logosynthesis. See Your Self. Be Your Self.
(Also available in German)

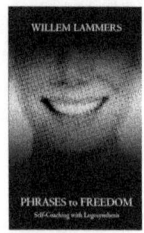

Phrases to Freedom. Self-Coaching with Logosynthesis
(Also available in German)

Logosynthesis. Change through the Magic of Words
Maienfeld, Switzerland: ias
(Also available in German)

OTHER BOOKS BY DR. WILLEM LAMMERS

Chefsache. Essays für Coaches und Manager/innen
Chur, Switzerland: Desertina.

The Energy Odyssey. New Directions
in Energy Psychology
Maienfeld, Switzerland: ias.

www.ingramcontent.com/pod-product-compliance
Lightning Source LLC
Chambersburg PA
CBHW051548020426
42333CB00016B/2149